Takhi The Wild Horse

Written by Corrigan Farly
Watercolours by Tsolmon Damba

Copyright © 2022 Corrigan Farly. All rights reserved. No part of this book may be reproduced or used in any way without the prior written permission of the copyright owner, except for the use of brief quotations in a book review.

ISBN: 978-1-7373454-1-1
Library of Congress Number: 2022902343

Website: moralofthestorybooks.com

Watercolours by Tsolmon Damba
Book Design by Victor Rook

Dedicated to Berkeley,
a wild horse in the making.

Look closely, C. Farly!

Foreword

Having faced extinction, Takhi, also known as the Przewalski Horse, has never been domesticated and is our world's last remaining wild horse. Takhi is the last of the wild horse lineage that so captivated our ancient ancestor's imagination they were persistently and majestically painted upon the cave walls of Lascaux (above), Chauvet, Altamira, and Santimamiñe beginning some 42,000 years ago.

Inspired by seeing the Takhi at the Washington, D.C. National Zoo, Mongolia, and the successful reintroduction of this magnificent horse back to the Mongolian Steppe, the Takhi is one of humanity's greatest against-all-odds conservation success stories.

Tsolmon and I hope this story and these modern "cave paintings" continue the awe and inspiration of our ancient human ancestors, so we, too, can gratefully live in an amazing and wonderful world where wild horses run free…

Takhi was born a wild horse, on a cold and windy day.

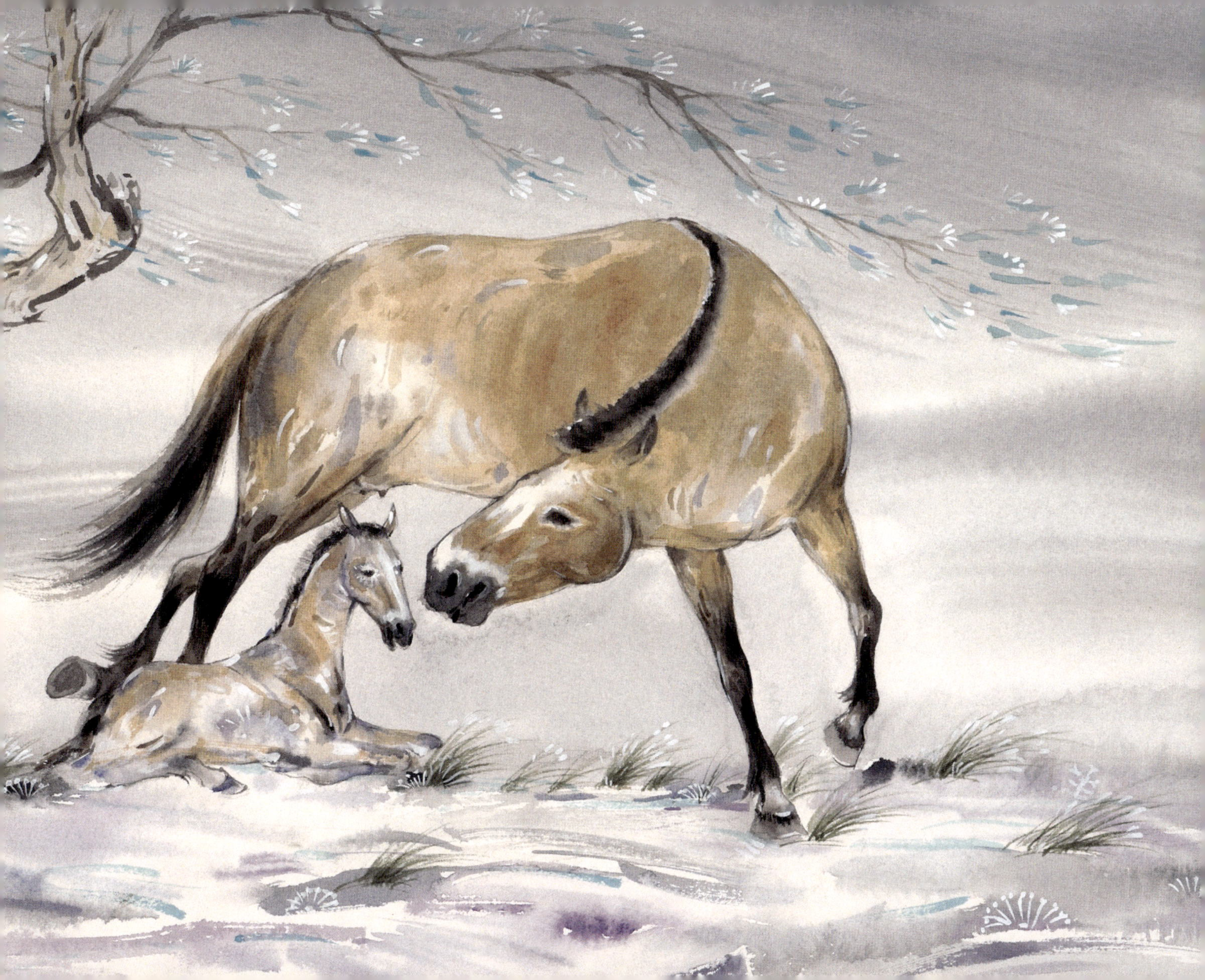

He was bucked and bit and stomped on,
that's how wild horses play.

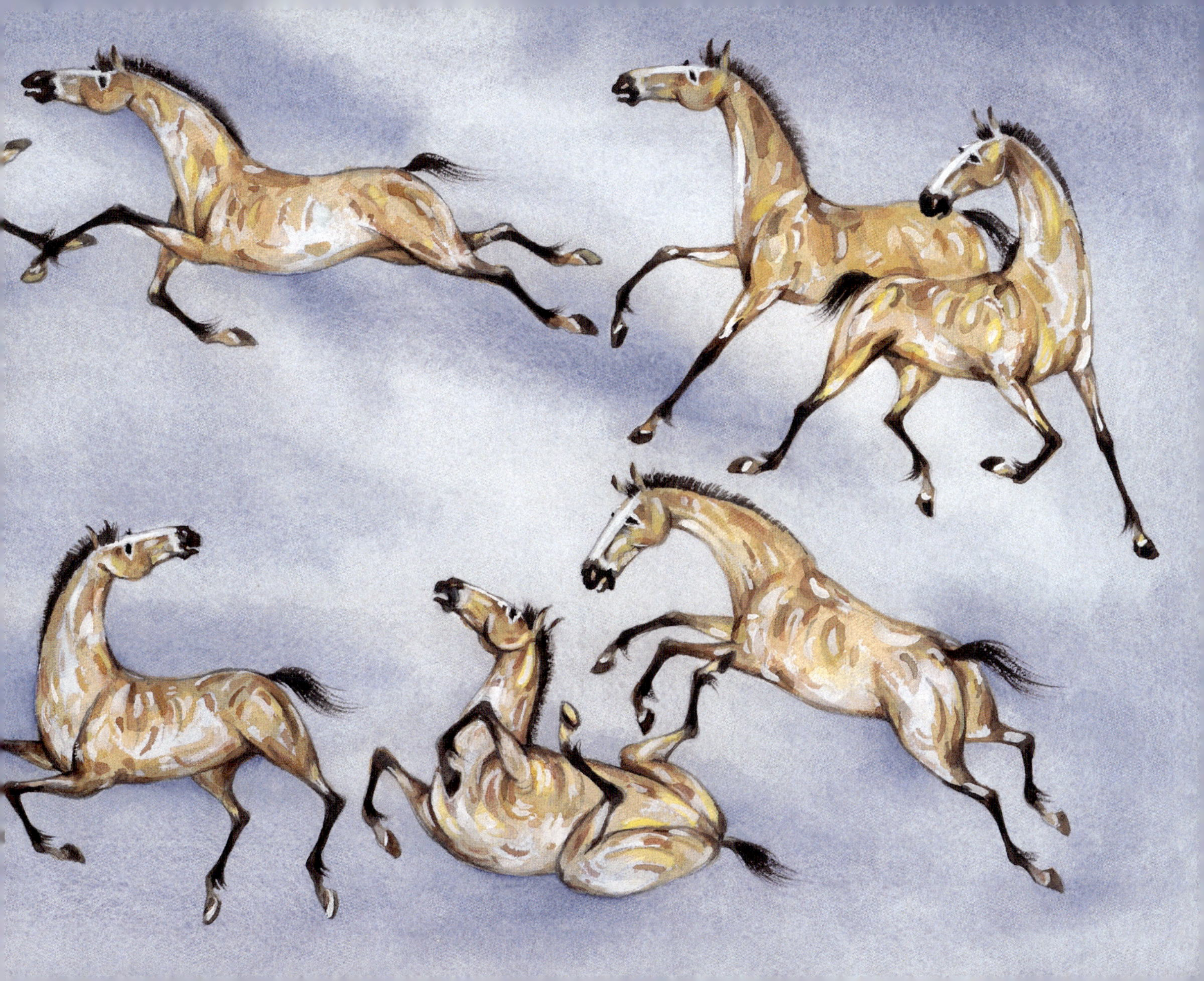

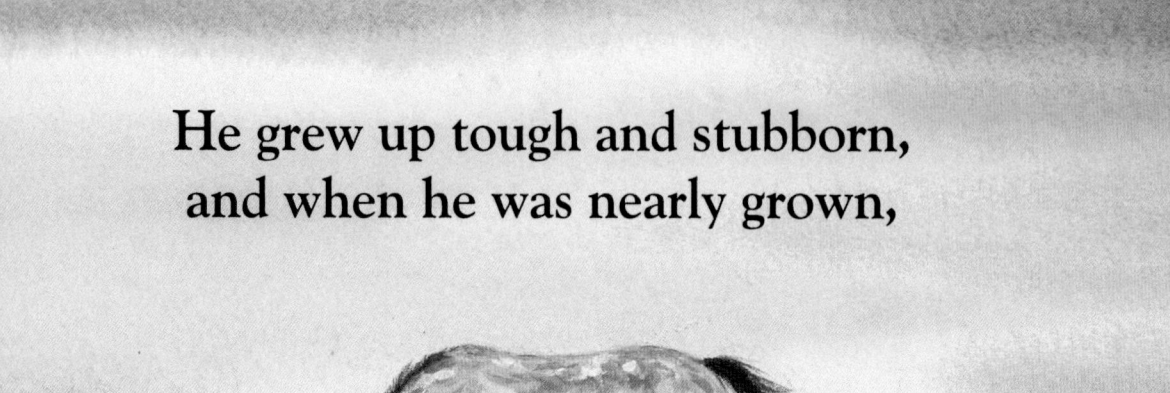

He grew up tough and stubborn,
and when he was nearly grown,

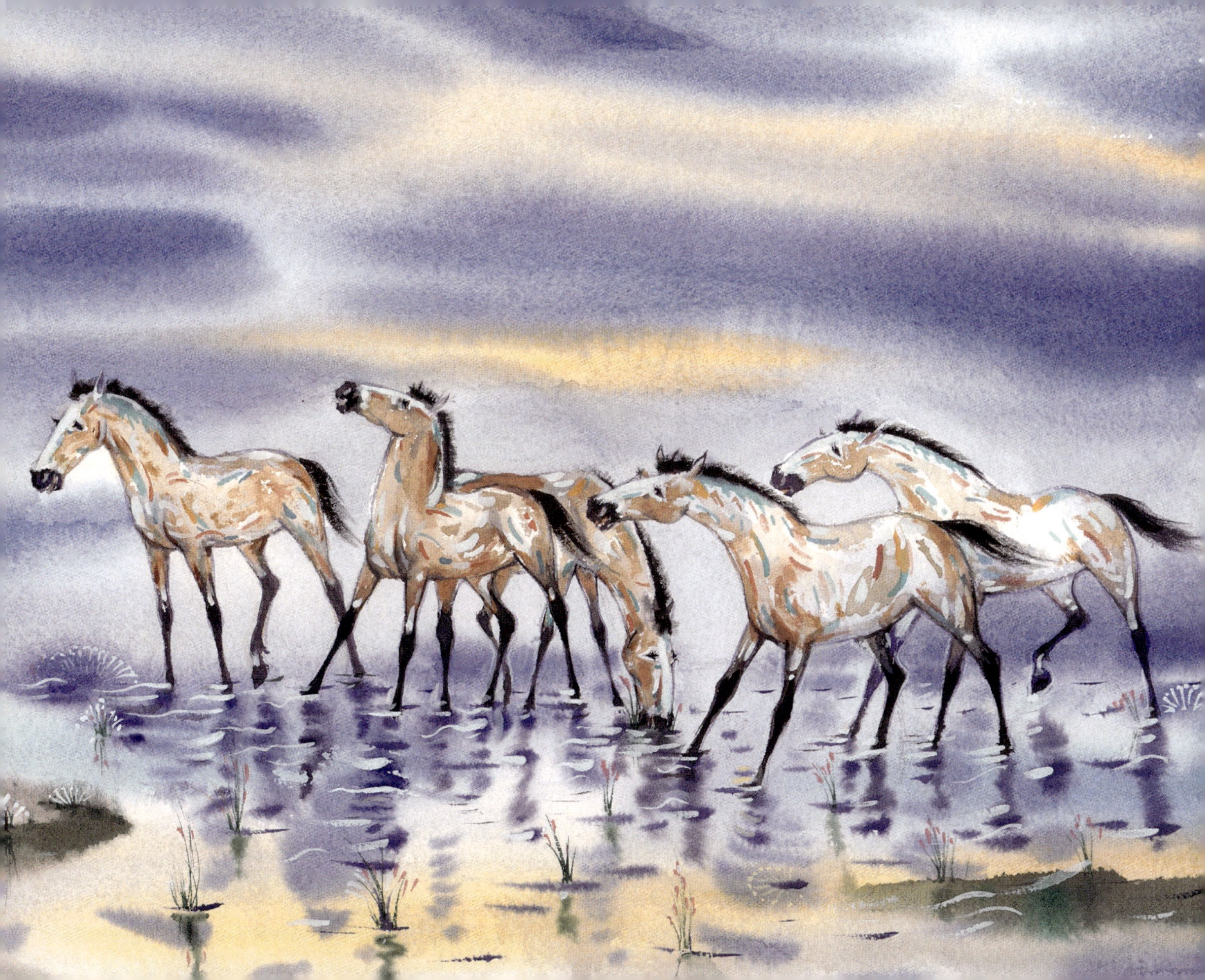

he was sent off into the wilderness,
where wild horses go alone.

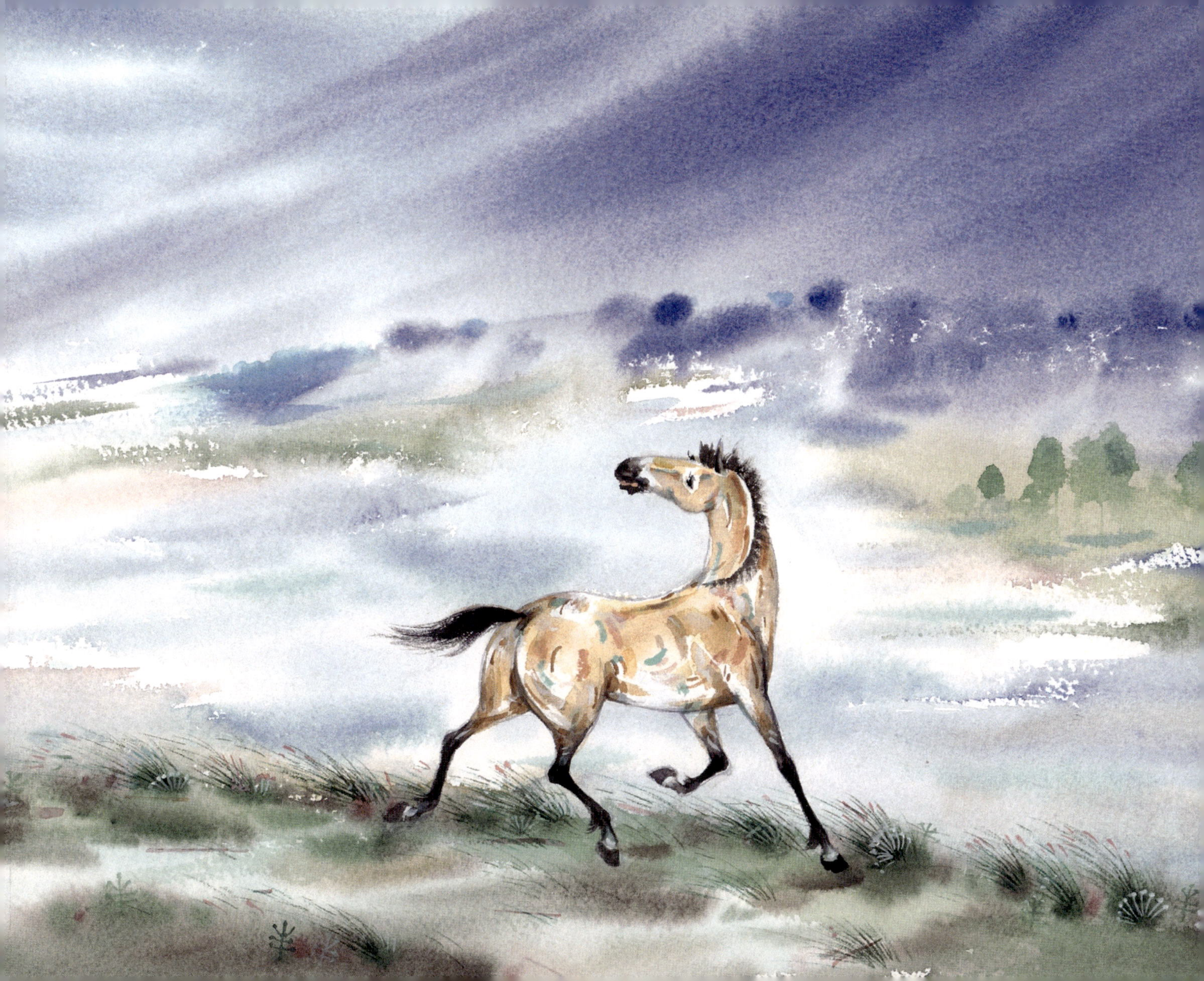

When food was scarce he went hungry,

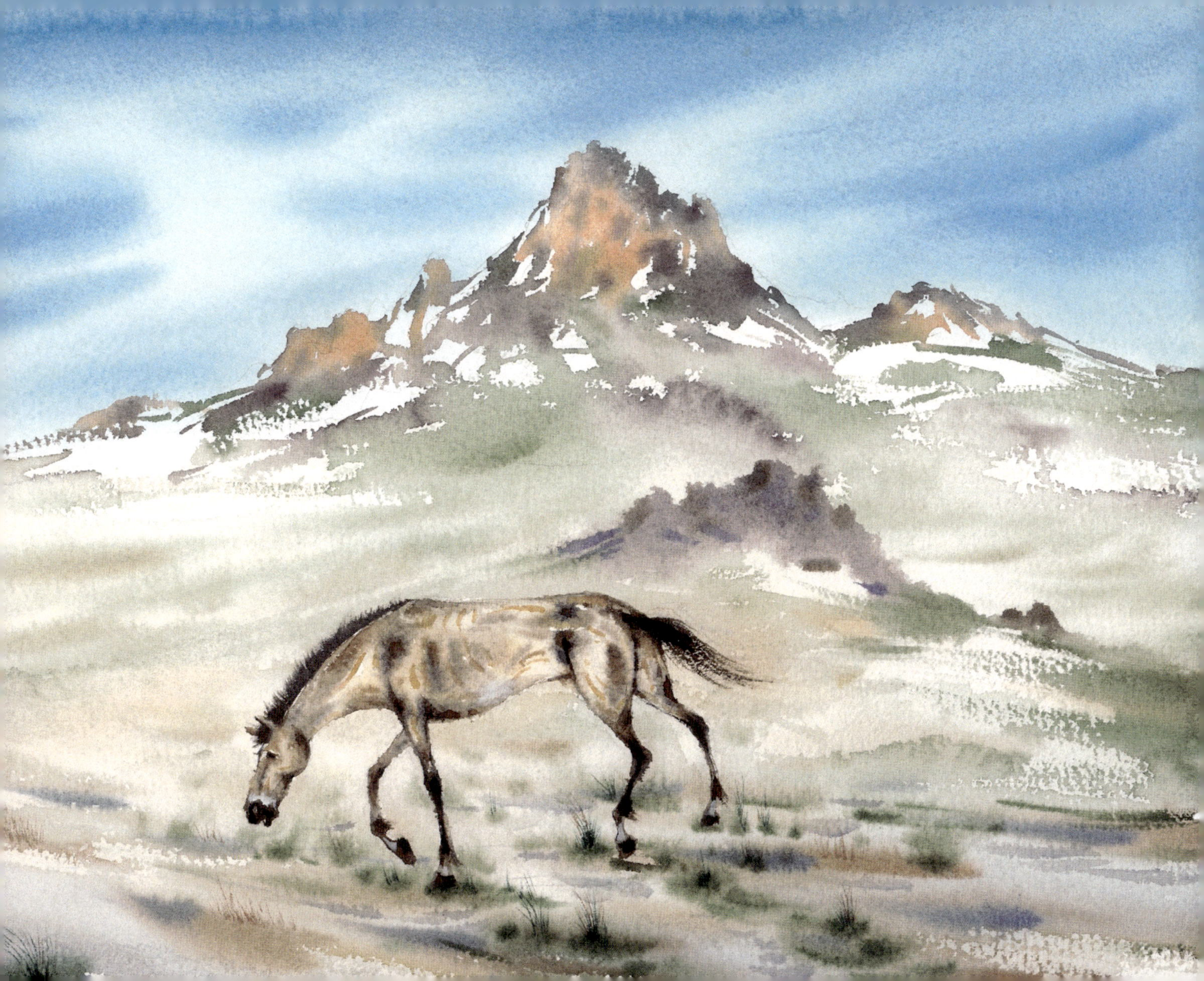

during drought he had great thirst,

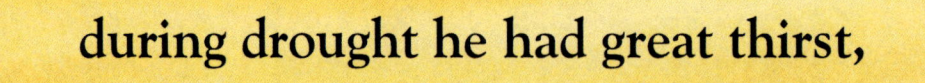

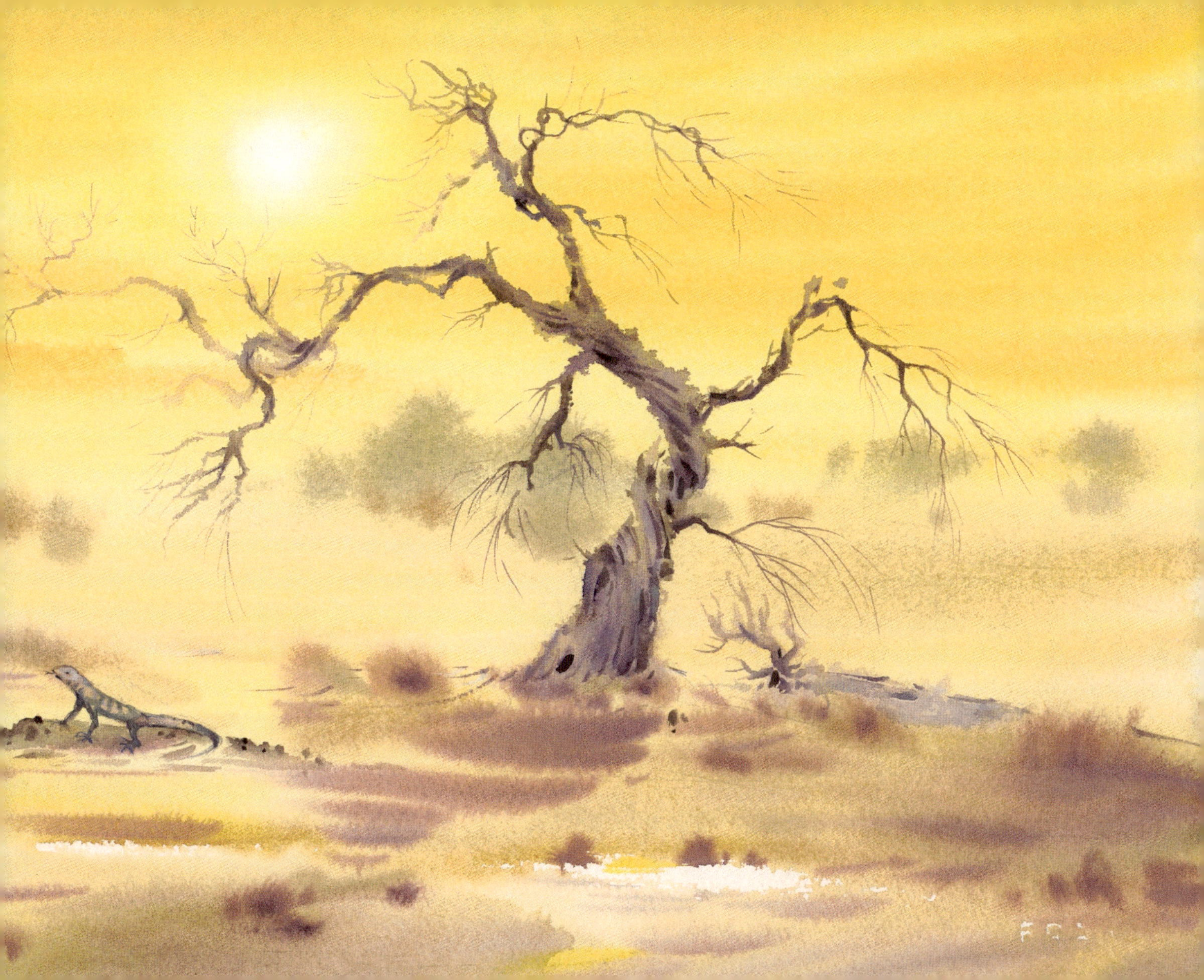

he was cold,

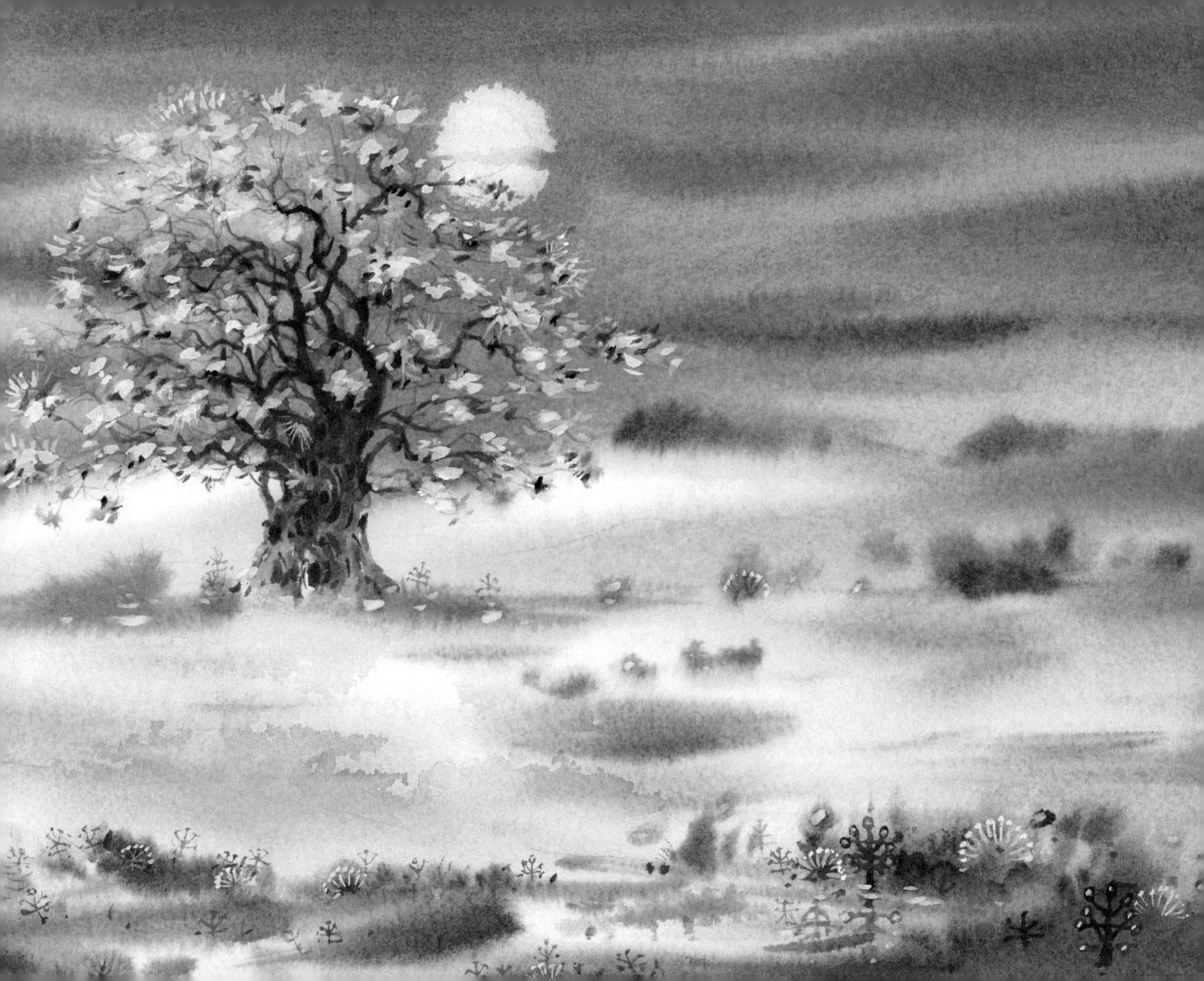

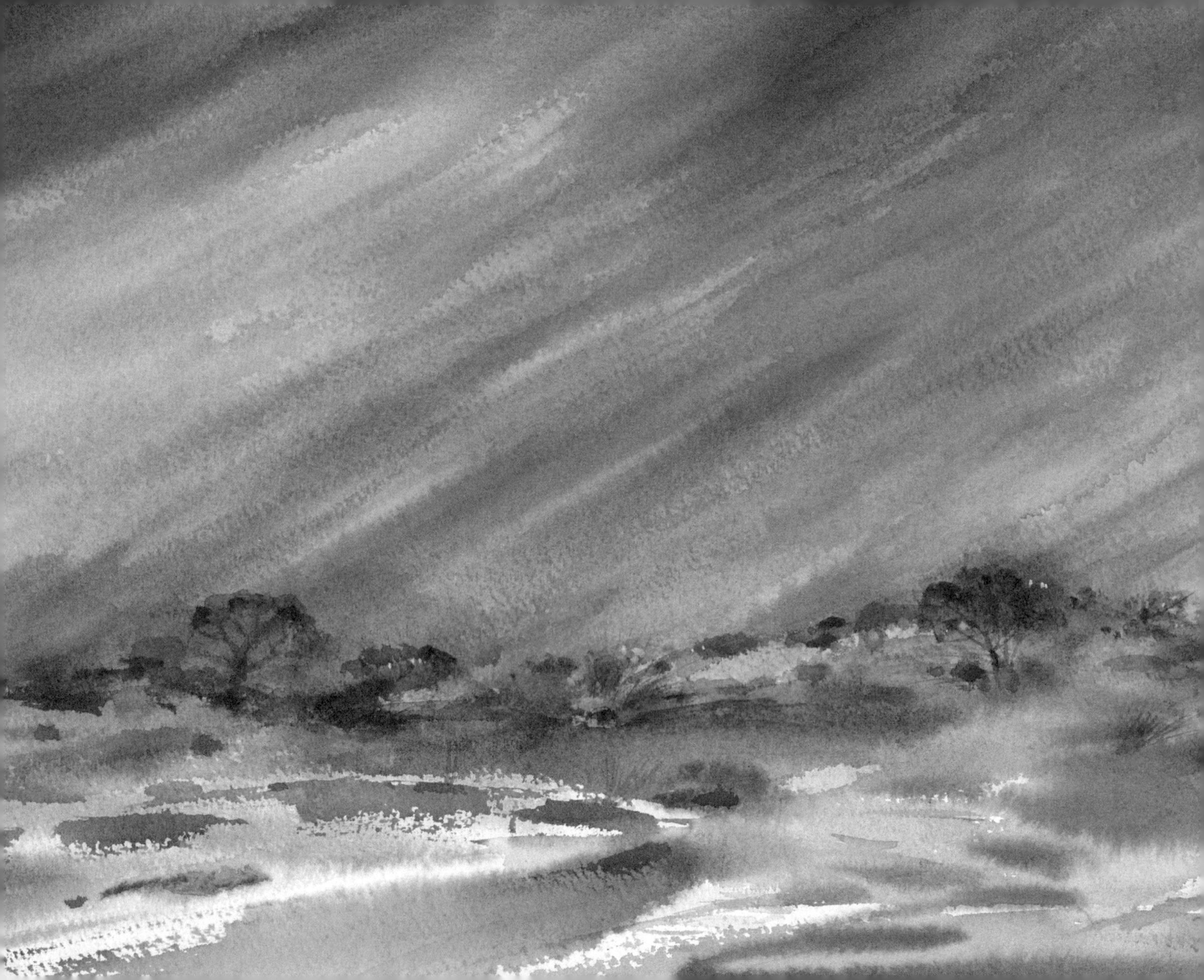

he got rained on,

but being chased by wolves
was the worst.

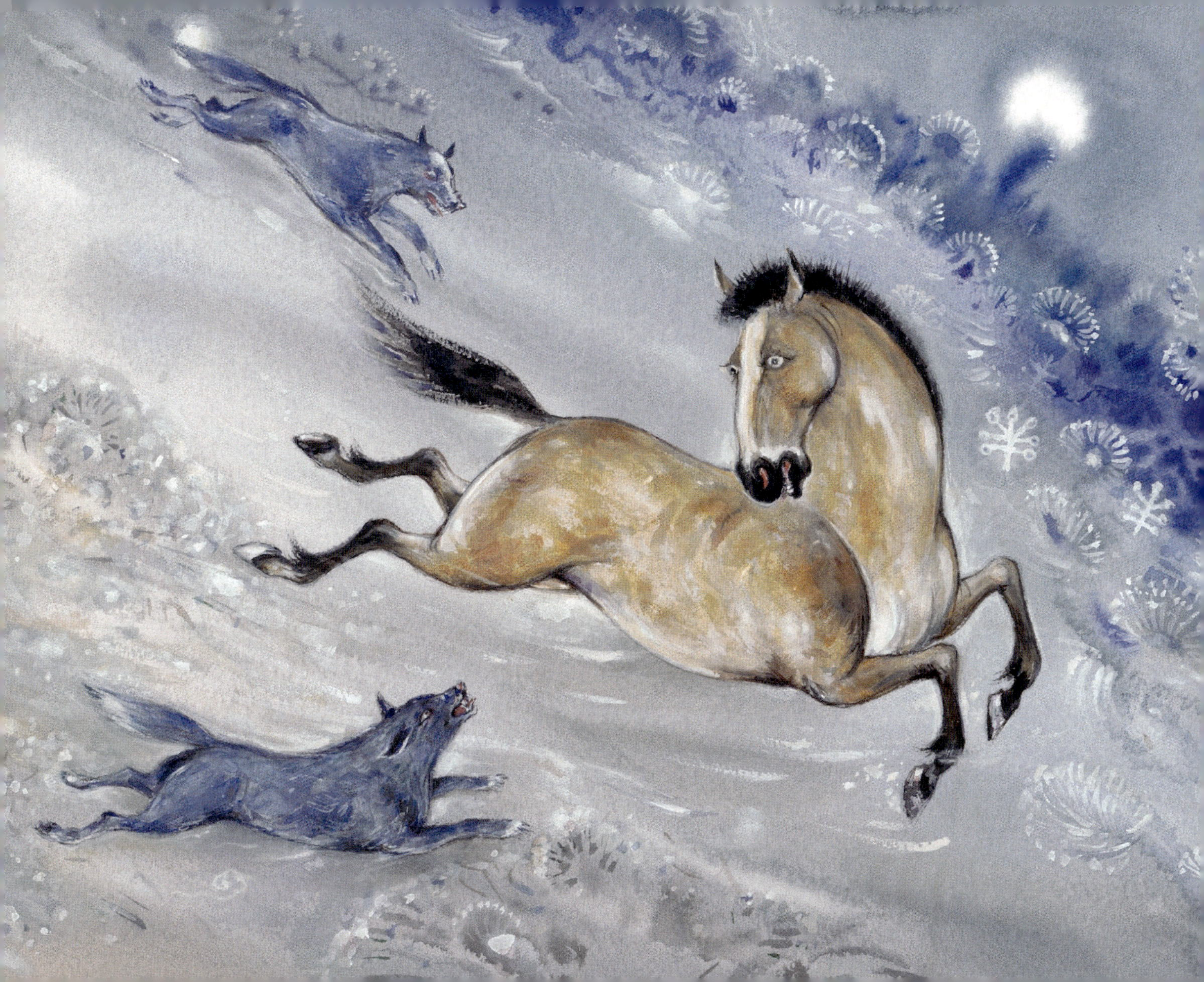

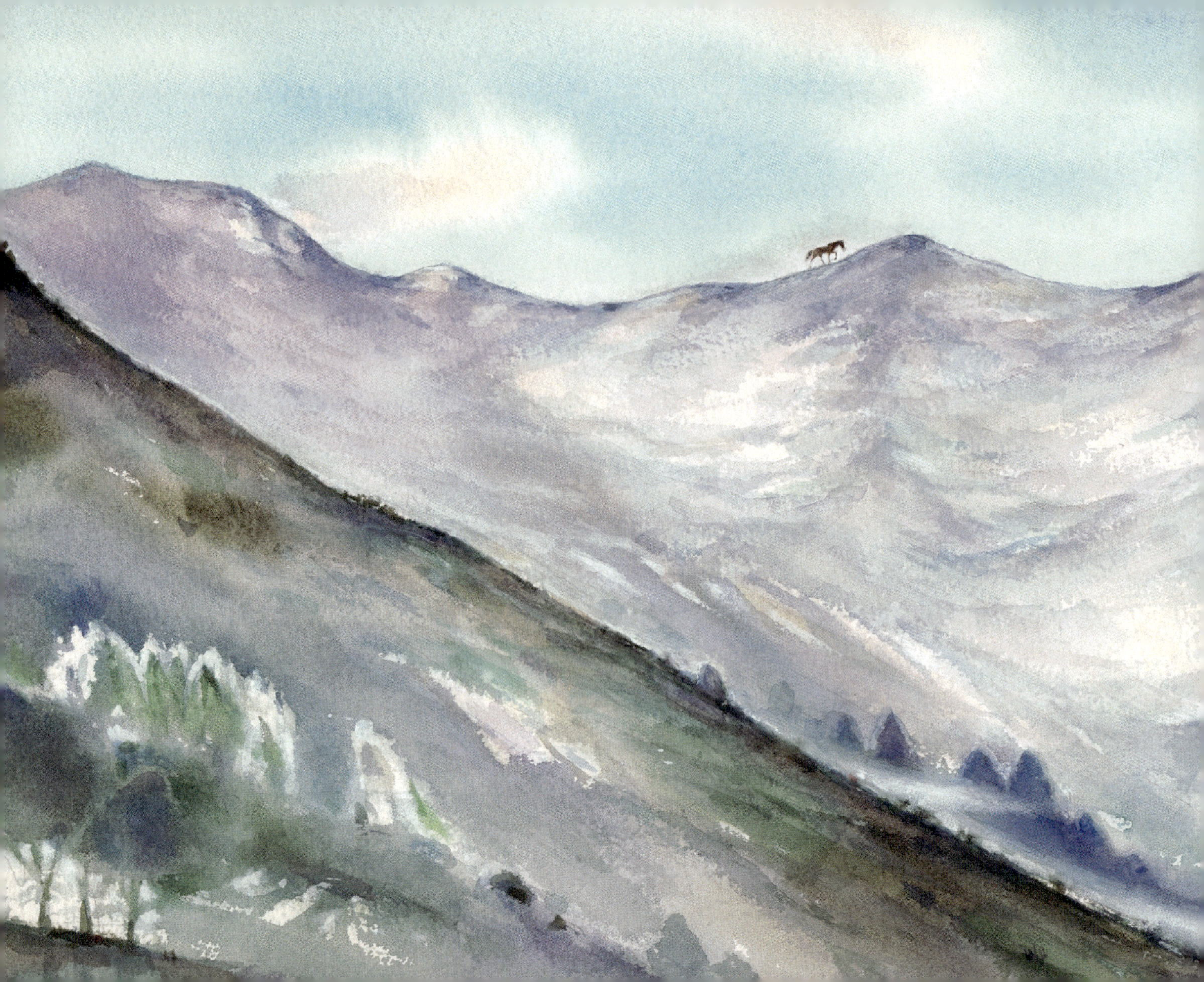

He struggled over mountains,

through the valleys,

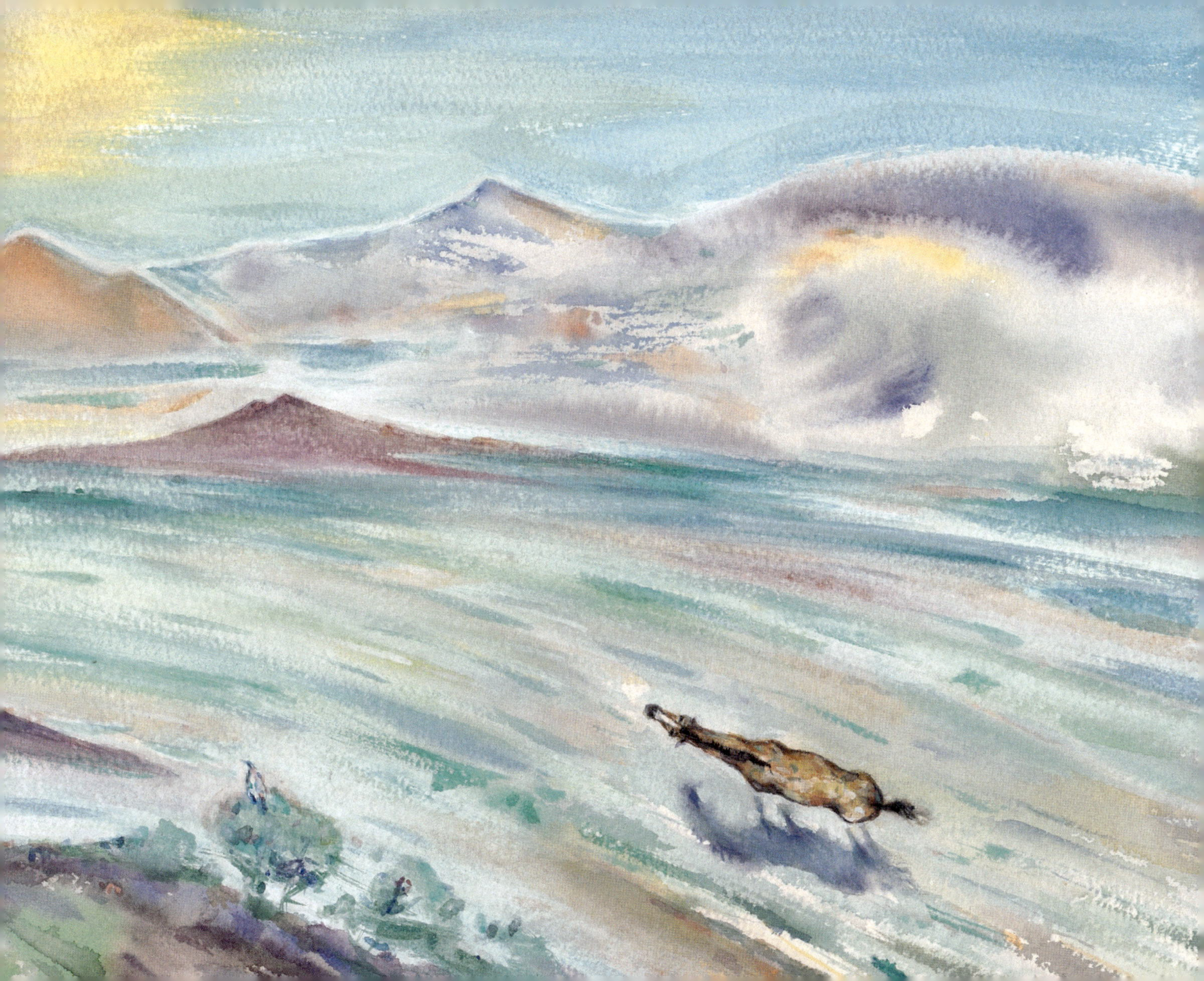

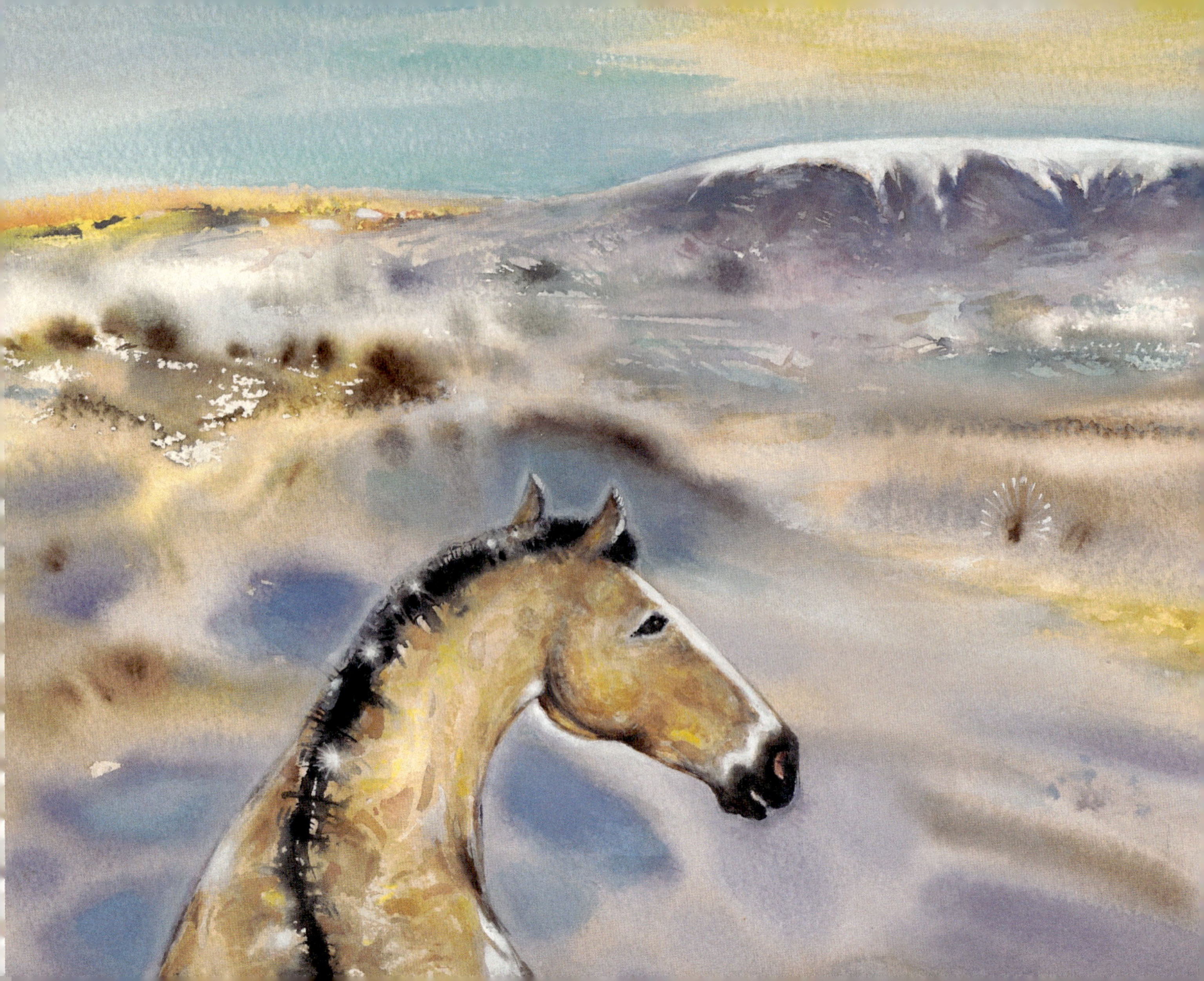

and there in a small, secluded glen,

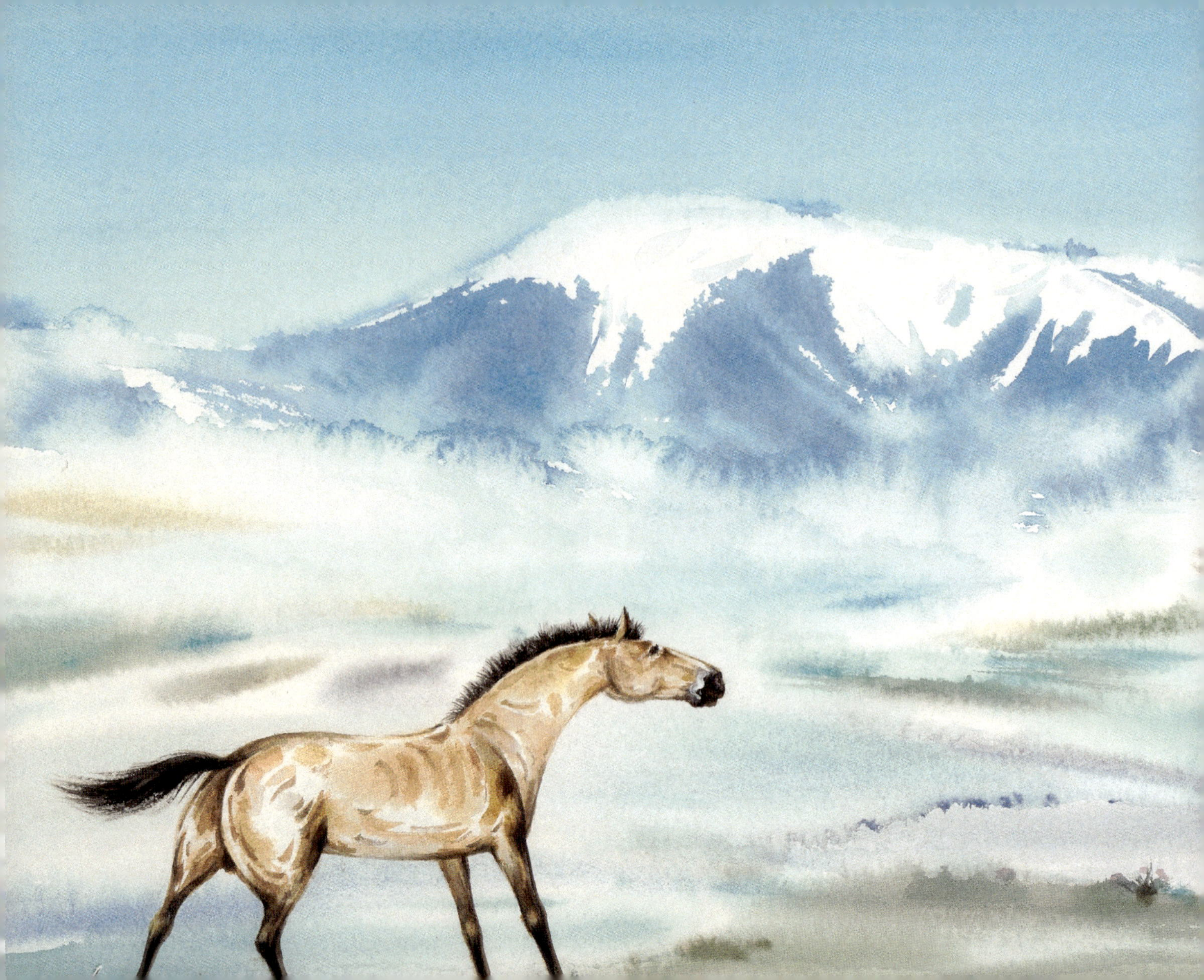

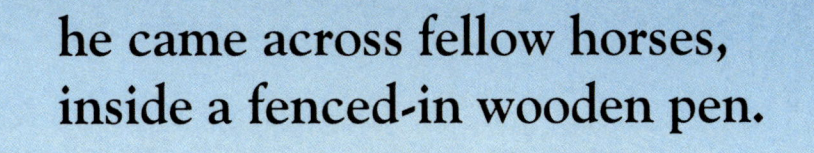

he came across fellow horses,
inside a fenced-in wooden pen.

The horses said to Takhi, "We are fed, given water,
protected from the wolves, the cold, the rain,
this is a safe and comfortable place to live your life…

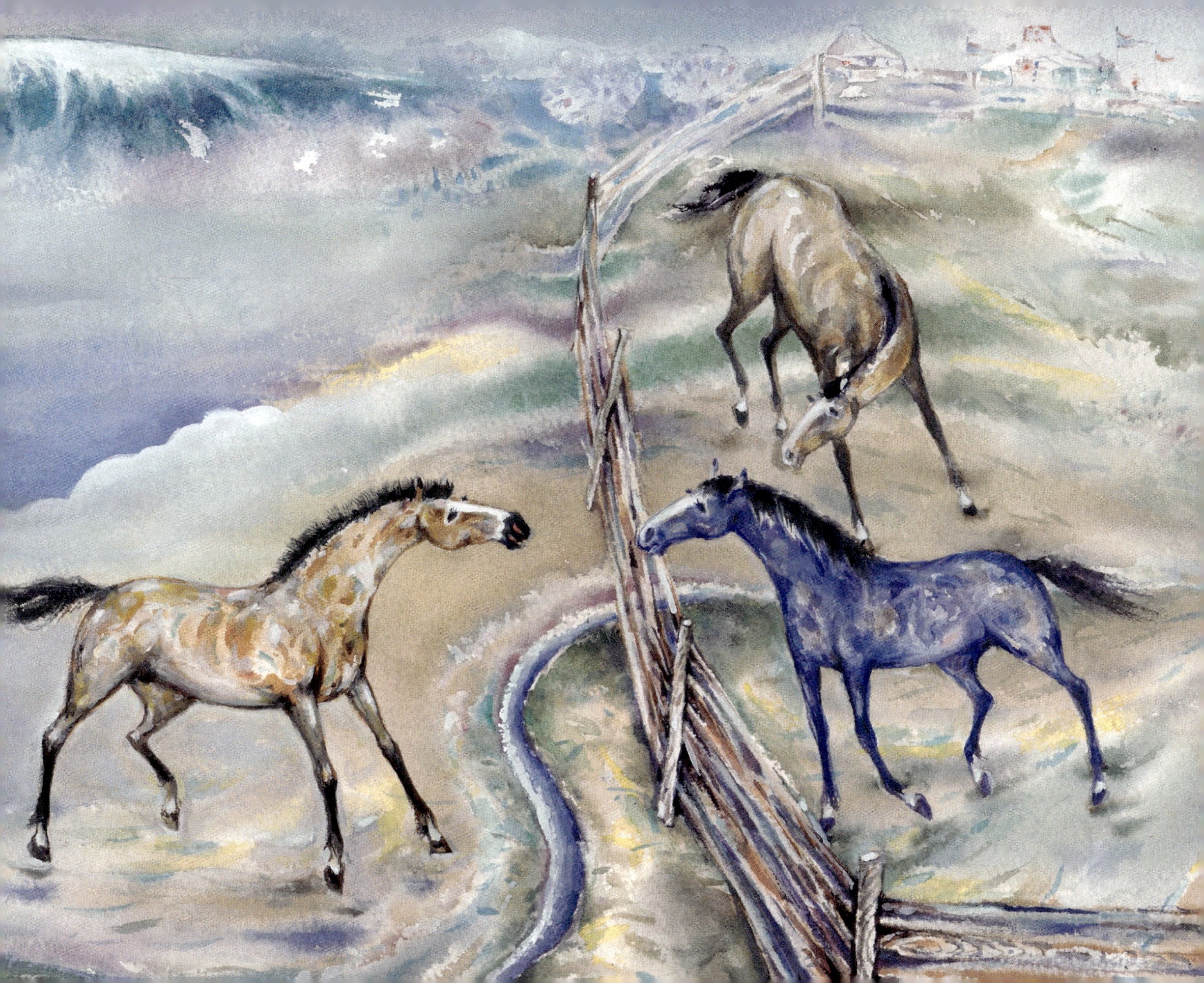

you should join us and remain."

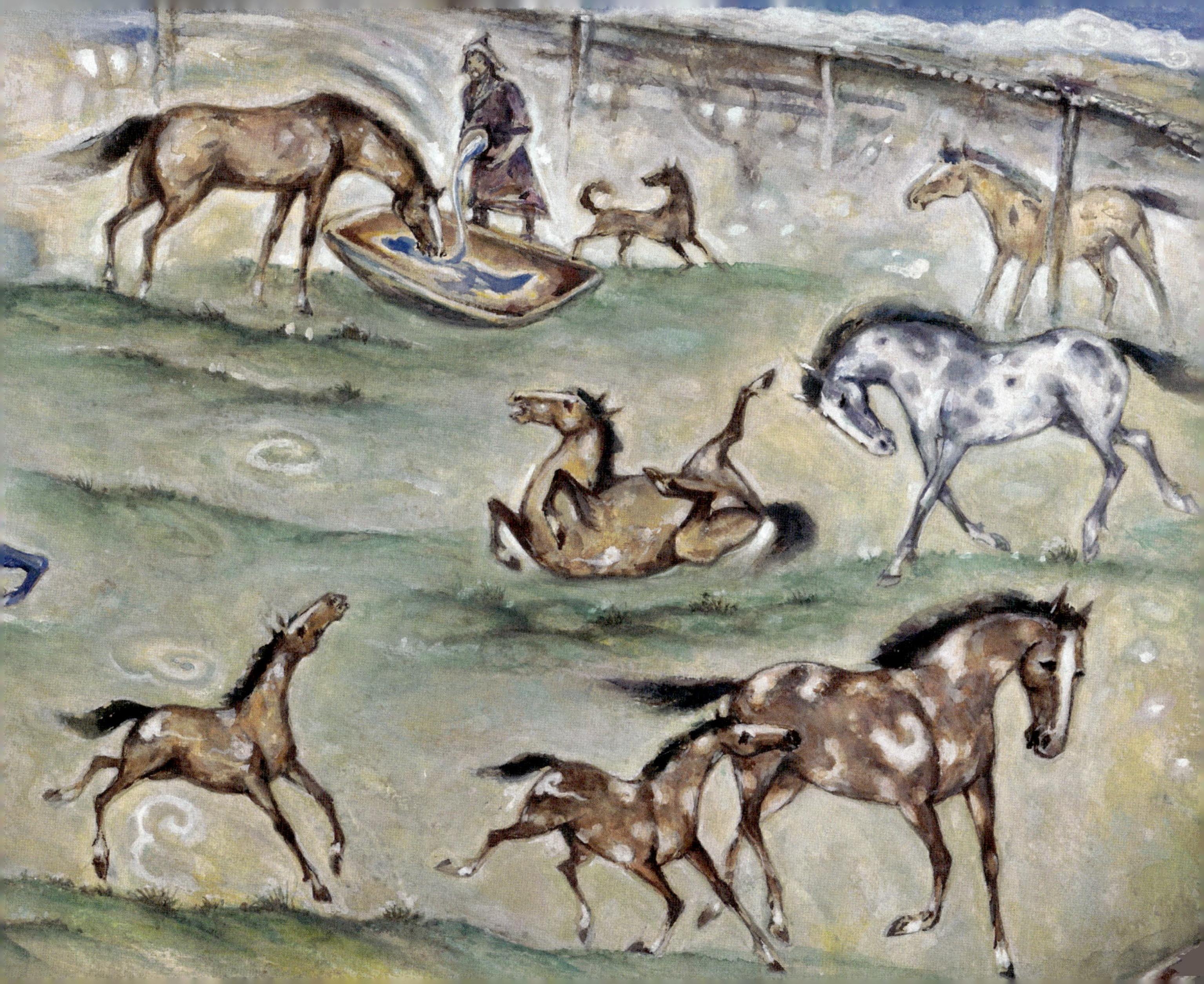

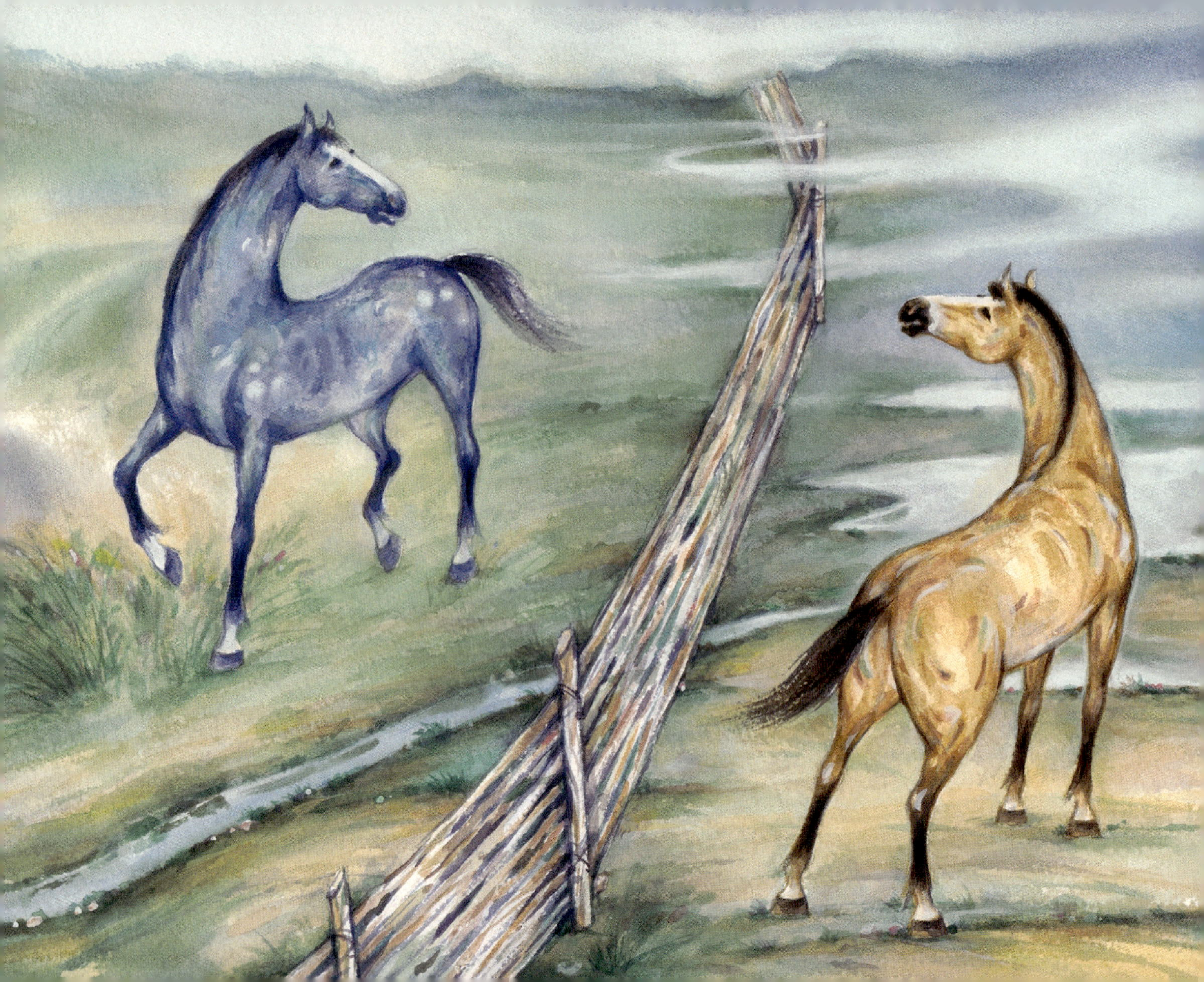

Takhi said,
"Fellow horses, everyone must choose their path,
and this may be your chosen course…

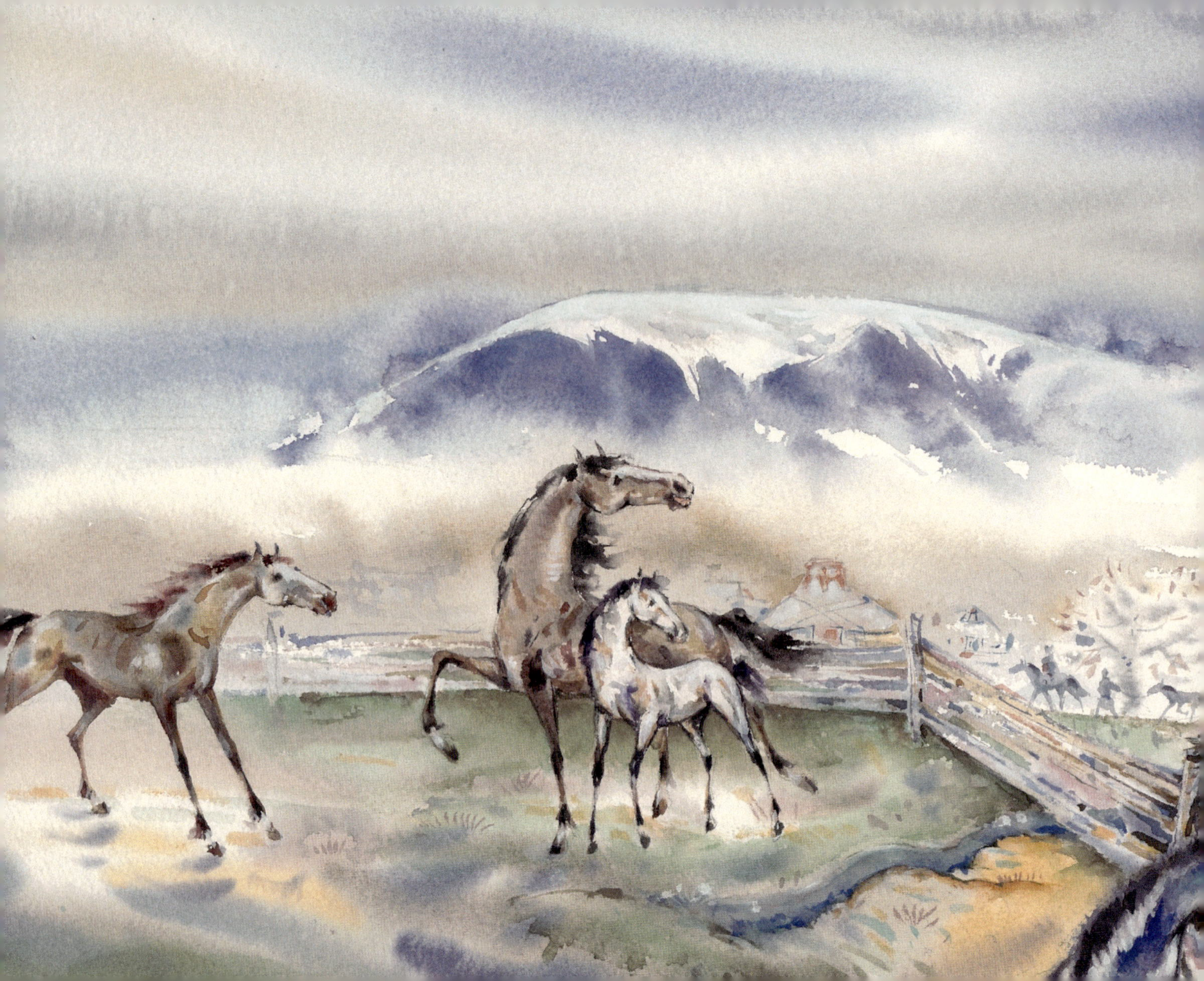

but stay is something I cannot do,
I am not that kind of horse.

For I will not be caged,

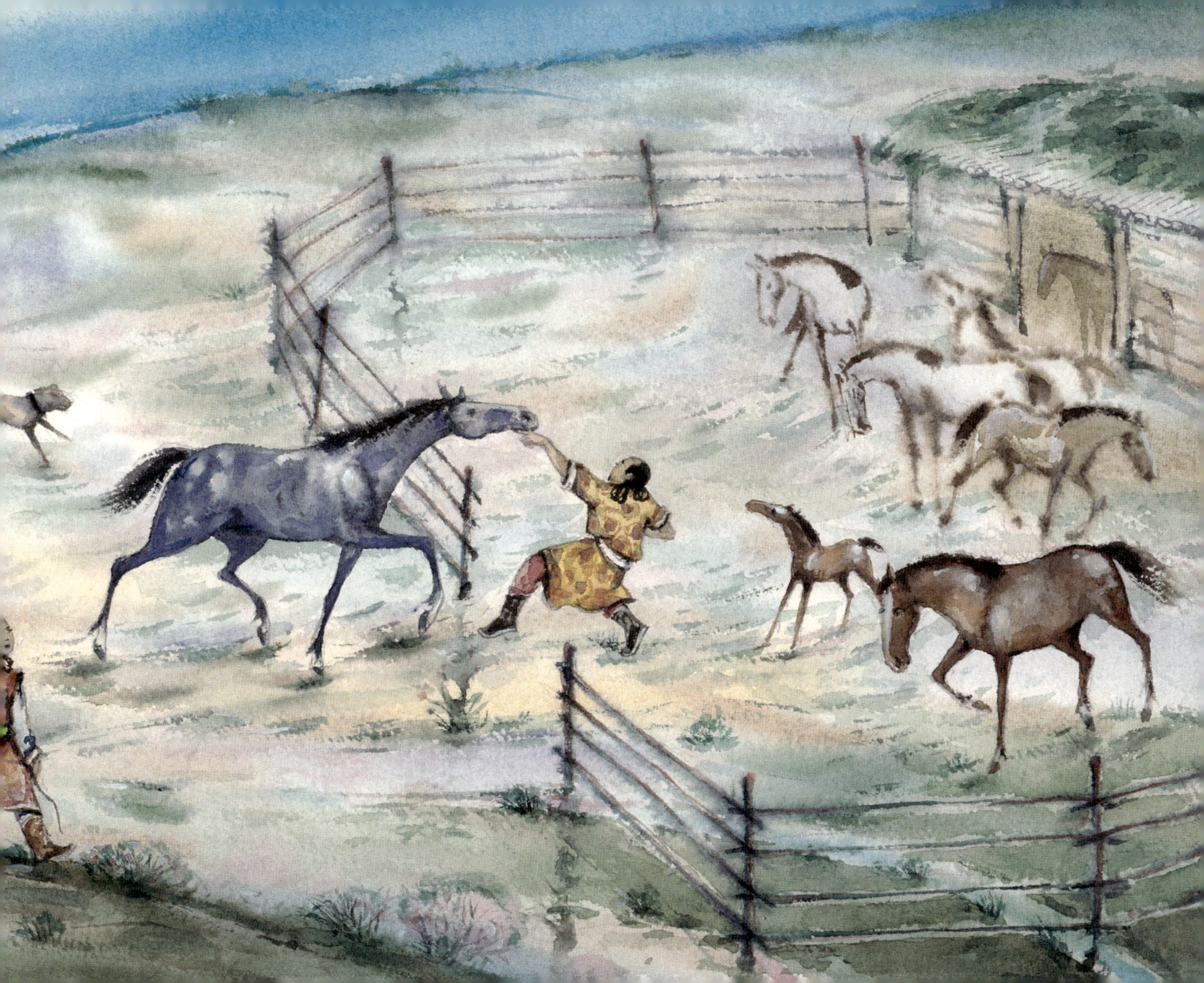

I will not be fed,

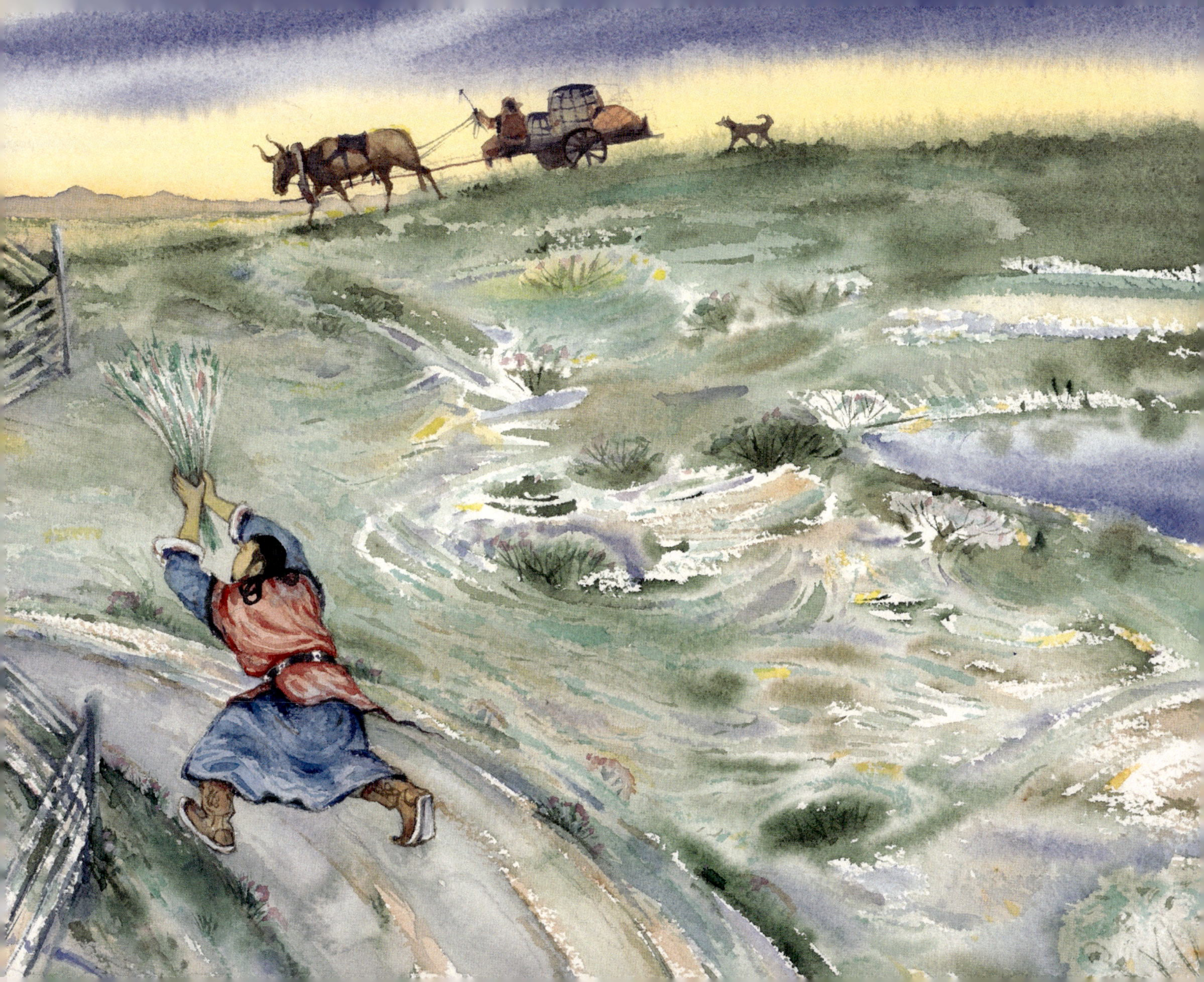

I will not be owned,

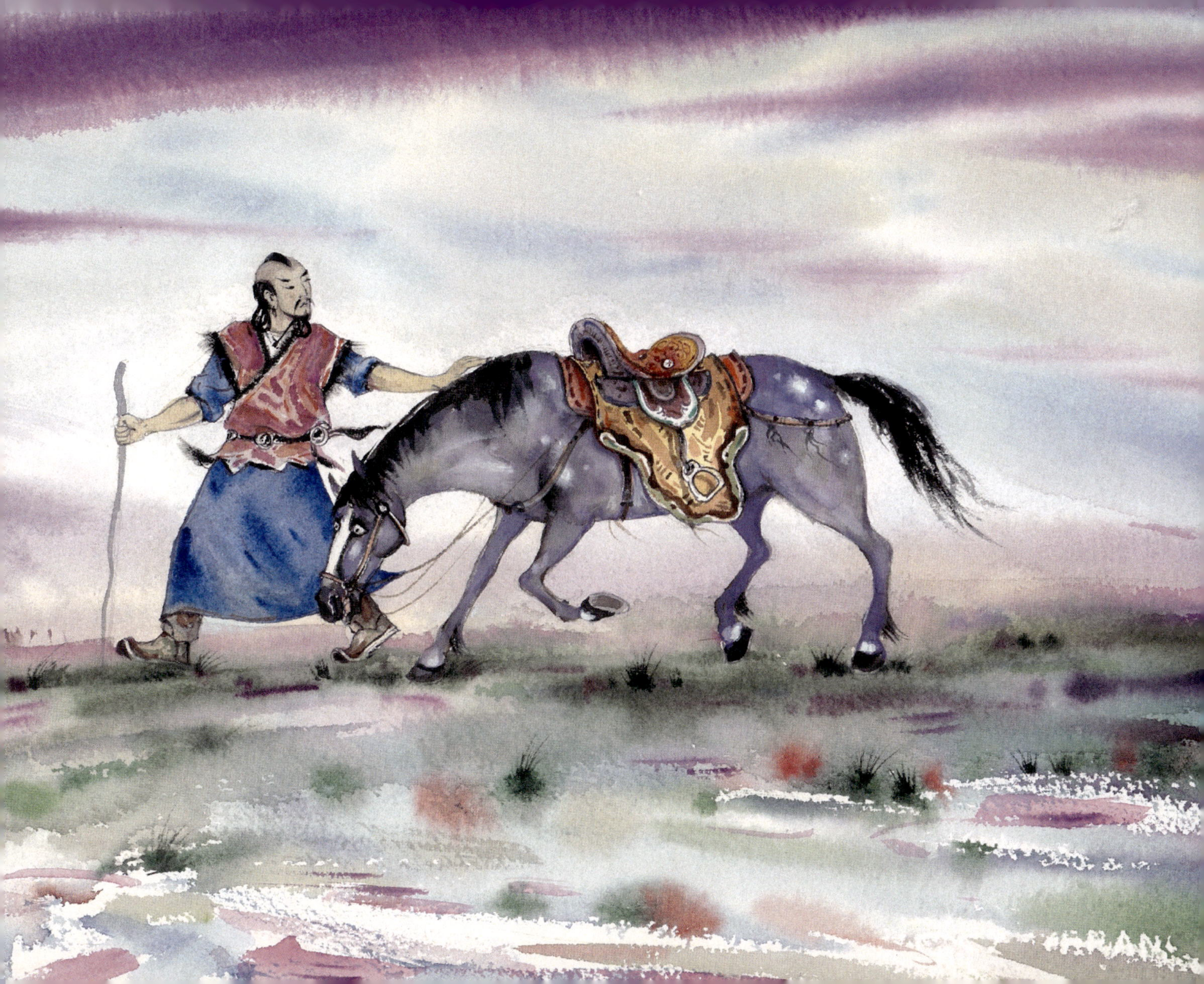

and I will not be led.

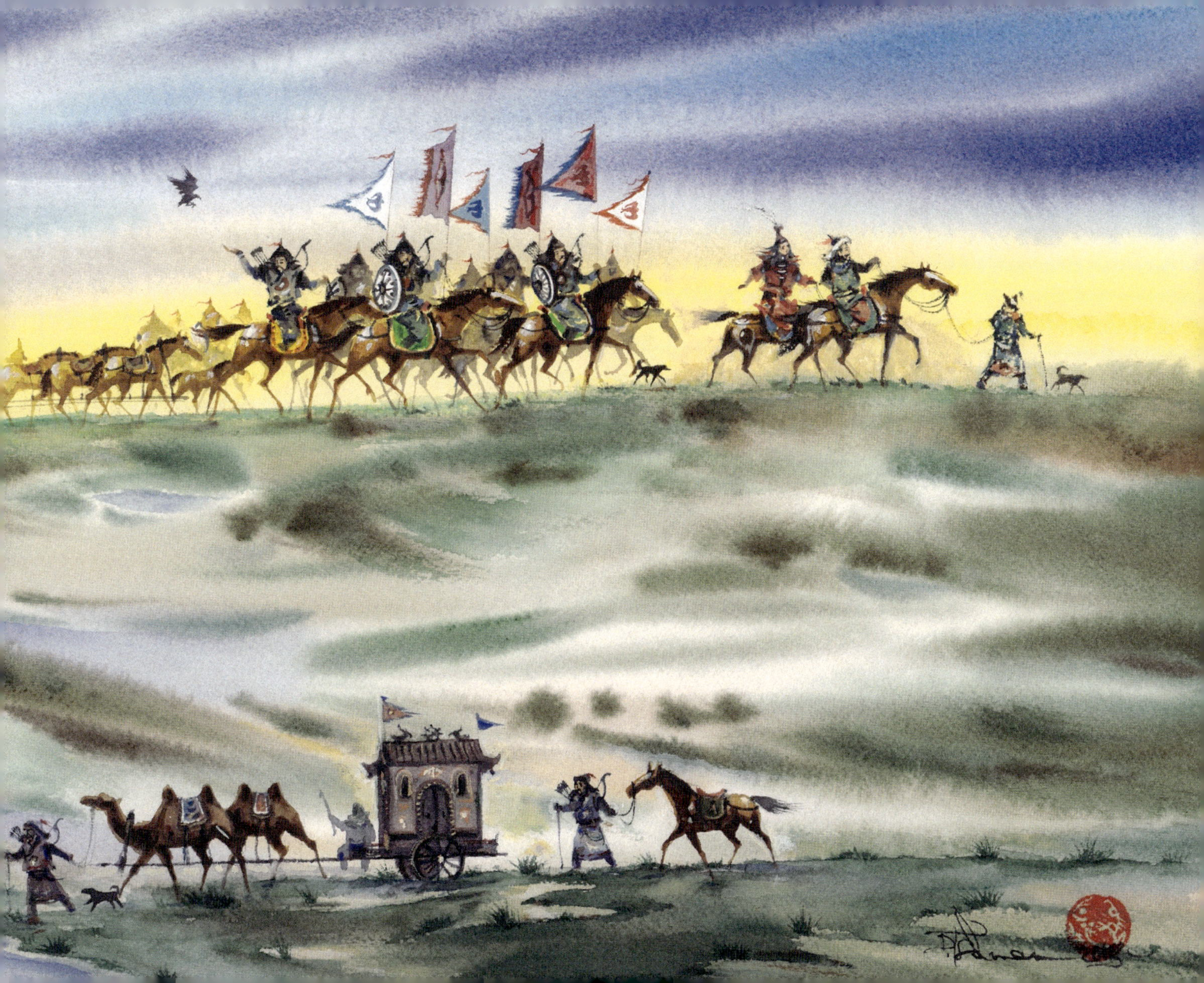

There are places I must travel,

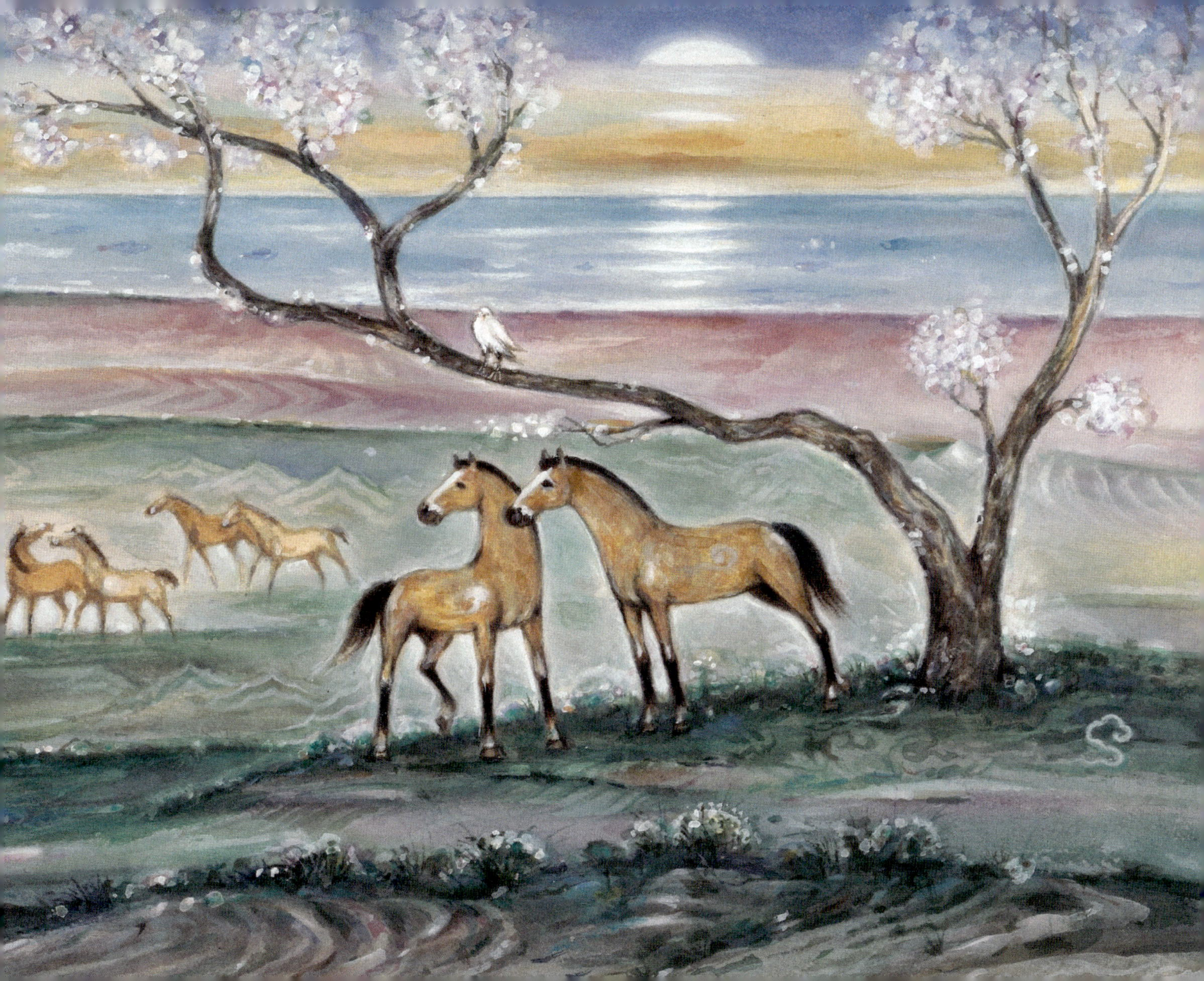

there are things that I must see,

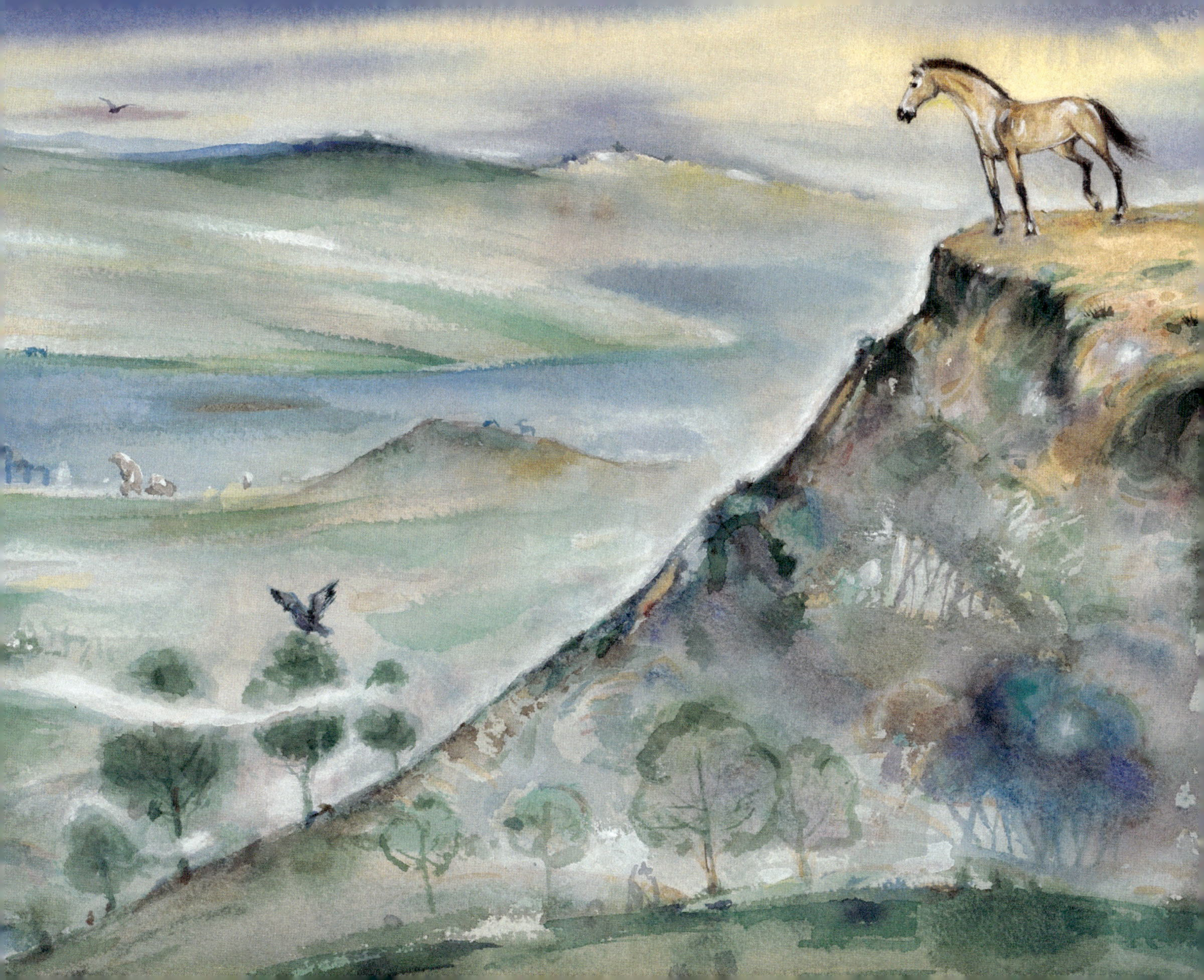

I am a Wild Horse,

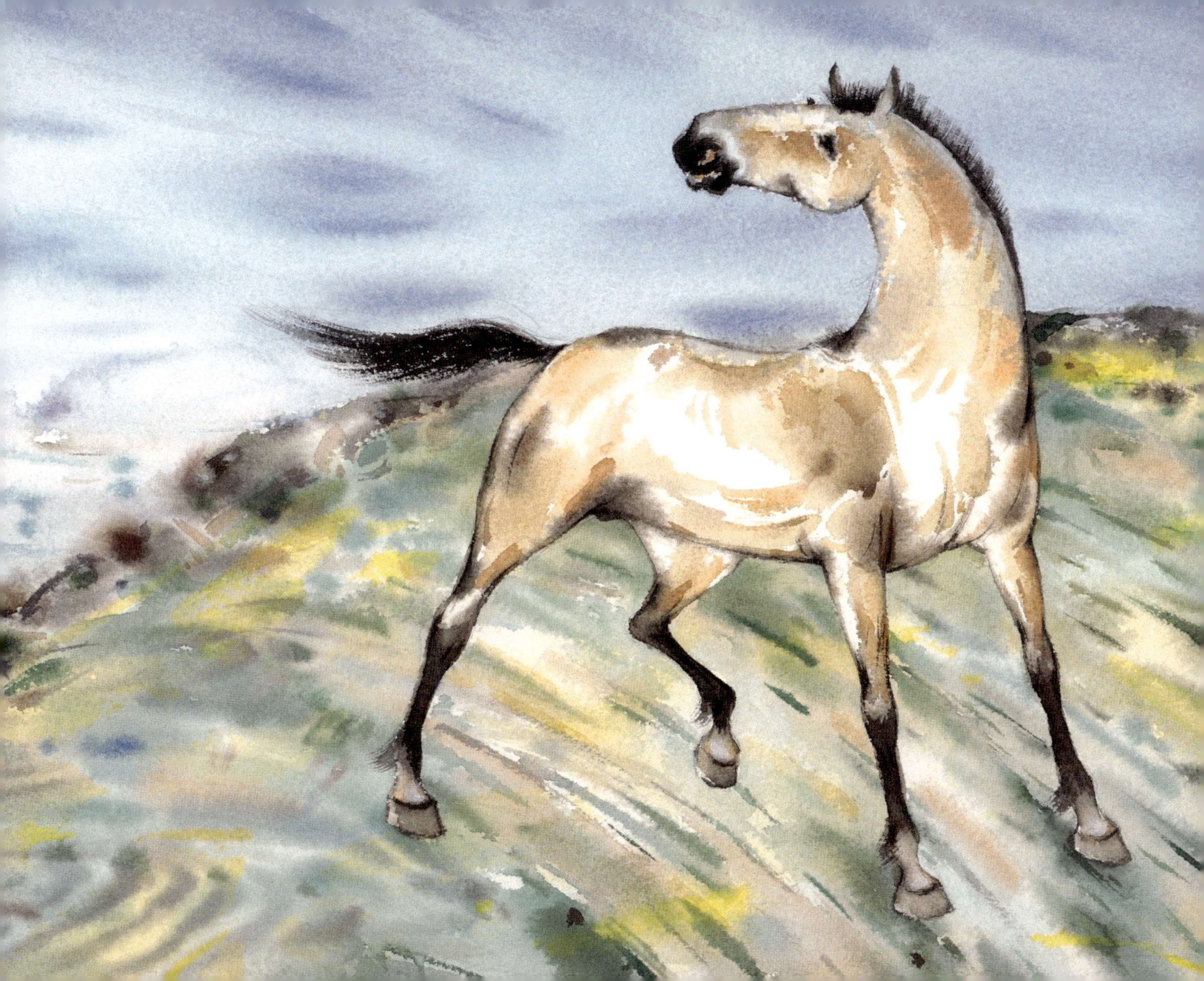

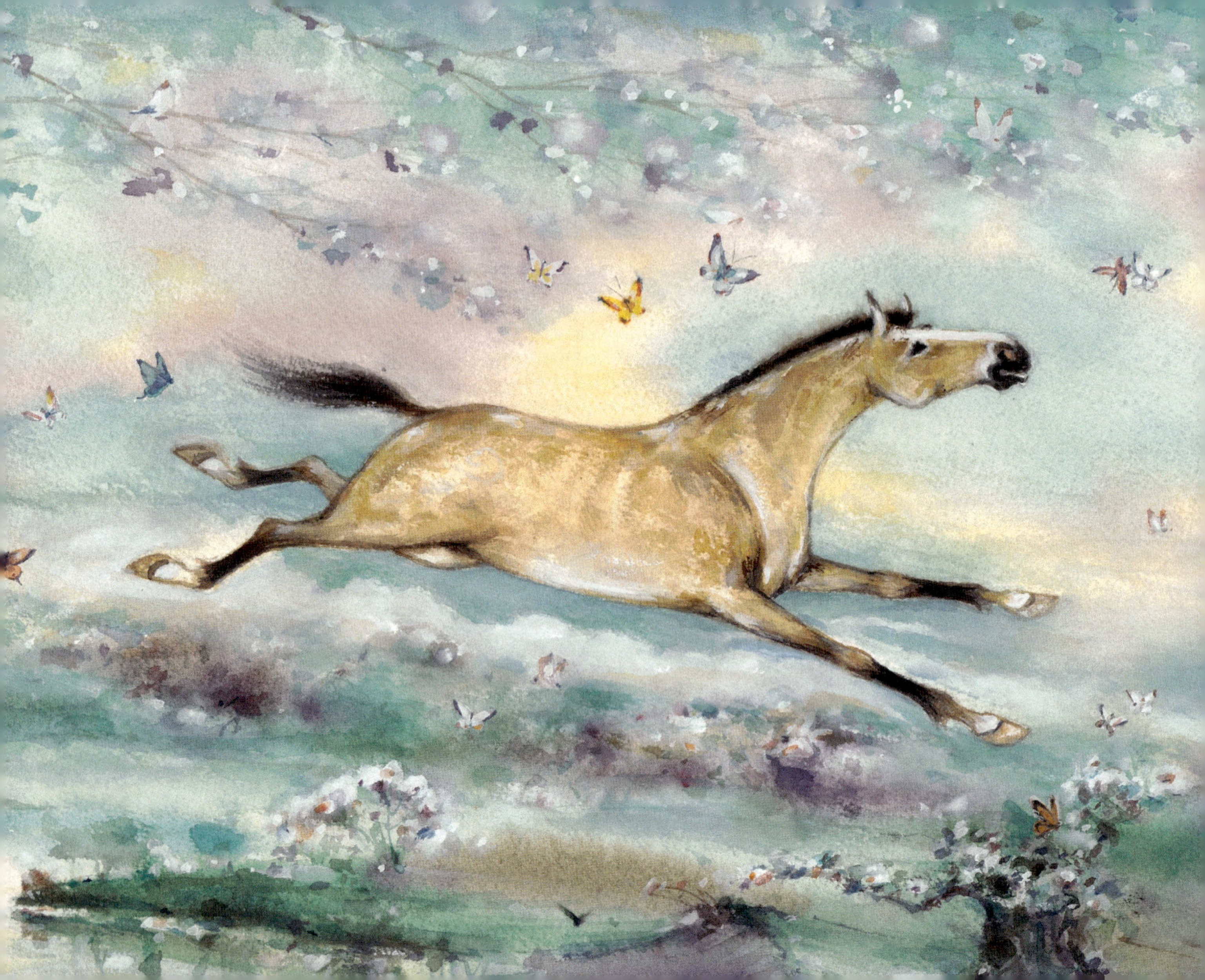

and Wild Horses…

Must Run Free!"

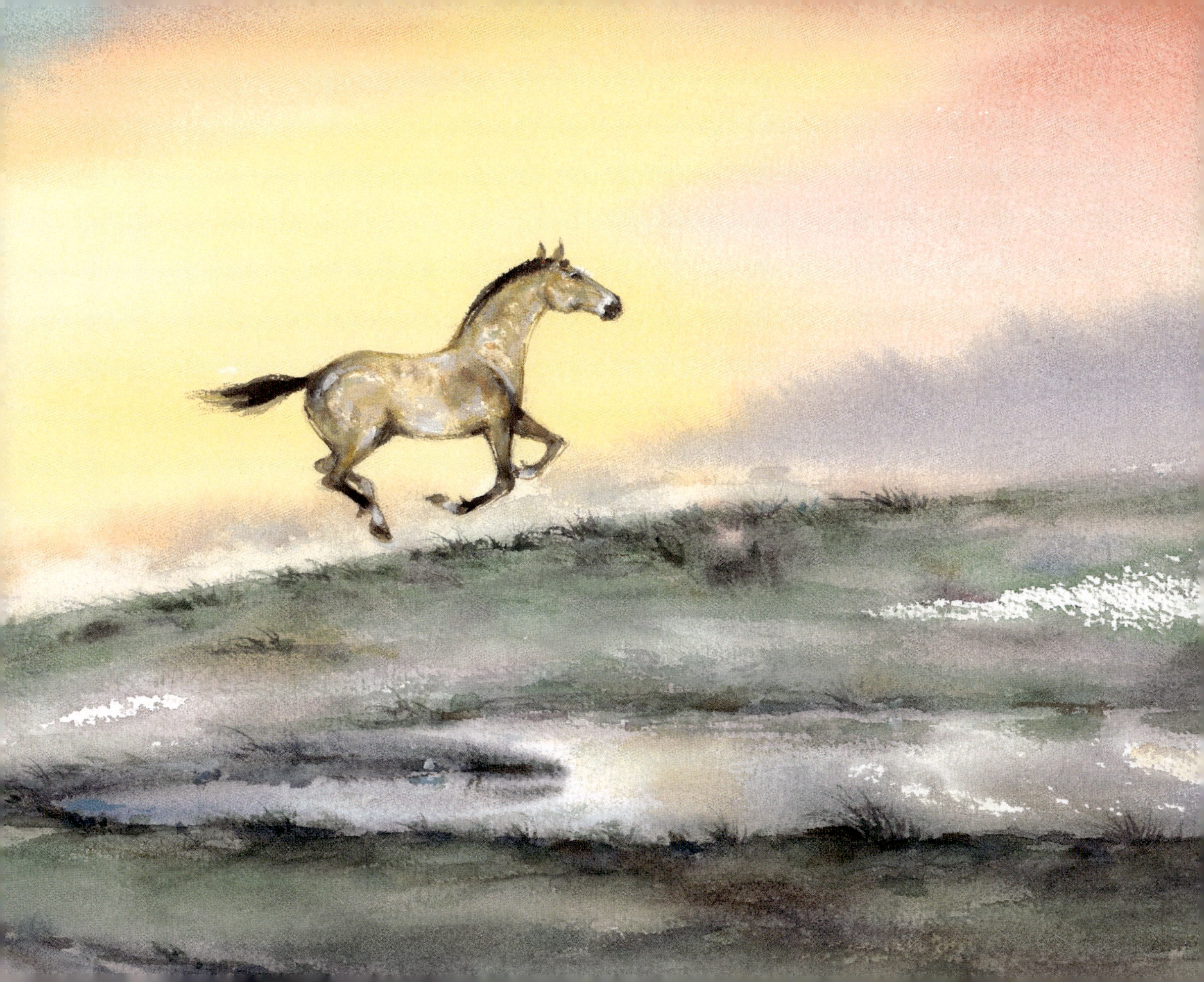

Author Bios

Corrigan Farly

Corrigan Farly loves writing picture books! He lives in Virginia with his wife, daughter and cat (who all seem to be wild…). He is incredibly lucky and grateful getting to make this book with his friend and great artist, Tsolmon Damba. Look for future books by Corrigan Farly and Moral of the Story Books at www.moralofthestorybooks.com.

Tsolmon Damba

Tsolmon Damba was born in Darkhan, Mongolia. He grew up playing on the picturesque banks of the Kharaa river surrounded by the mountains of Kherkh and Mount Shirhentseg, gazing at the blue ridge of the majestic Noyon Uul in the midst of the beautiful, serene countryside of Mongolia. At three years old Tsolmon started drawing and painting. His unmistakable talent and creativeness caught everyone's attention, especially his grandmother Baga Ajaa. When the time came, Baga Ajaa packed up her grandson and brought Tsolmon to where his talent could flourish: the capital city of Ulaanbaatar. There, among the hustle and bustle of city life, she enrolled her grandson in the Mongolian College of Fine Art, where he graduated and would later teach.

Tsolmon was first immersed in ancient Mongolian art, especially the prehistoric cave and rock drawings as well as the indigenous art of the Bronze Era. At the Mongolian Cultural Heritage Center in Ulaanbaatar, Tsolmon worked as an artist and helped restore historical works of art. While painting, procuring and restoring the Center's priceless works and artifacts, Tsolmon found his *raison d'etre* (life's true passion) and earned his master's degree in Traditional Mongolian Painting.

From the banks of the Kharaa river, to Ulaanbaatar, to worldwide exhibits and art shows, to teaching demonstrations at the Smithsonian's Freer Gallery of Art, the Arthur M. Sackler Gallery and the Museum of Natural History in Washington, D.C., Tsolmon's unique talent comes full circle in *Takhi the Wild Horse*. Here, Tsolmon beautifully depicts Takhi living wild and free back in their native Mongolian countryside.

Made in the USA
Middletown, DE
02 January 2024